Grandparents & Young Children with Autism

Susan Louise Peterson

Grandparents & Young Children with Autism

Susan Louise Peterson

COPYRIGHT

CONTENTS

PREFACE

Being involved in early childhood assessment for autism and developmental delays has opened the door for me to find out about the unique perspectives that parents and grandparents bring to the assessment process. Family make-up is different and each family has certain struggles and challenges that are unique to their personal family needs and situations and these issues may impact how a program is designed or implemented for a child or grandchild with autism. The book, ***Grandparents & Young Children with Autism*** focuses more on the grandparent's struggles and issues related to caregiving a child or grandchild with autism. The resources are available, but it is hoped that this book will provide some additional guidance for grandparents in their journey with understanding a grandchild who has autism or needs to be assessed to find out if the child has autism.

PROLOGUE

Autism is a frightening topic for many families because of the different ways children and grandchildren present with the characteristics of the disorder. It is particularly stressful for many grandparents who are quickly put into situations where they are asked to be a caretaker or guardian for a young grandchild that may be showing signs or symptoms of autism. Grandparents who may have been away from educational settings for years are now put back into a world that has different special education laws, education procedures and new programs that have just been developed in the last few years. ***Grandparents & Young Children with Autism*** is written to help grandparents navigate through some of the issues that they may be faced with as they start the early childhood assessment process to find out if the grandchild is presenting with autism characteristics.

ACKNOWLEDGMENTS

I would like to thank the many people who have helped me understand the numerous perspectives of autism from a variety of points of view. This help has come from medical professionals, educators, therapists, parents and grandparents and children and grandchildren who have shared their unique experiences related to autism.

A big thanks is given to my daughters who point out to me that I should always consider different perspectives and points of view. My husband has always been a wonderful support in writing and helping me with the technology aspects of writing that sometimes frustrate me as an author. My family is wonderful and I thank each of them for their support and kindness in my personal writing journey.

INTRODUCTION

Grandparents today are faced with many challenges, but one of the biggest challenges is when they are asked to care for grandchildren with autism. This is new territory for many grandparents who are unfamiliar with autism related disorders or the characteristics of autism. However, there are so many resources available to understand autism and find community resources. The book ***Grandparents & Young Children with Autism*** was written to help explore this grandparent journey with understanding autism. Part of the book explores early childhood autism assessment and the issues that may occur during an autism educational eligibility testing process. There are also discussions related to practical issues such as a grandchild covering his or her ears and sickness examples that may mimic autism. The final chapter provides a nice overview of going through a multi-team autism assessment and some of the issues that may surface during the evaluation process. It is hoped that the book, ***Grandparents & Young Children with Autism*** will help grandparents with this challenge and gain a better understanding of the grandchild with autism.

CHAPTER 1

GRANDPARENT JOURNEY WITH AUTISM

Grandparents may find themselves on a new journey into the world of autism. They may discover the grandchild they are raising or helping to raise has autism. It is a little tricky for some grandparents who were raised in an era when childhood disabilities were not openly discussed. Years ago, a relative may have been a caregiver or watched a child with a disability in the back quarters of the house. Often times in the past, a child with a disorder or condition did not attend social functions outside of the home. However, a new awareness of disabilities has arisen in our society. Now families with children who have special needs or have autism are searching for ways to make life more enriching no matter what type of condition or disorder impacts a child's life.

There has been a sharp rise in the number of children diagnosed with autism. More and more people in their later years may be involved in raising or helping to care for a child with autism and various other delays or conditions. There are both areas of concern as well as strengths that can be identified between grandparents and the grandchild or grandchildren with autism. One strength is in finding the similarities and understanding the differences between the grandchild with autism and the grandparents related to various issues in life.

Health Issues

Sometimes the issues of the grandchild with autism and the grandparents have both similarities and differences. For example, grandparents may have numerous doctor's appointments for general health and specialized problems along with possible vision and hearing issues. The grandchild may also have a series of medical and school related type of appointments for immunizations, hearing exams, vision tests, nursing examinations, speech therapy and school psychologist's evaluations. Some grandchildren with autism may have specialized applied behavior therapy to help the child practice play, communication and social interaction experiences. Juggling medical and health related appointments for both the grandparents and the grandchild can be difficult in relation to scheduling, transportation and the organization to meet time demands and family responsibilities.

Stress Issues

The grandparent may deal with emotional issues and stress if grandchildren are coming into the household as a change in the family structure. In some situations, grandchildren have been raised by the grandparents from birth and the grandparents may have been involved in all of the medical appointments and diagnosis of autism from a physician at an early age. However, some grandparents are surprised to find out that they are suddenly in a parenting role again and raising a grandchild with autism characteristics. The grandchild may also be dealing with stress from changing to a different house or place, loss of contact with parents, friends or significant others in his or her life.

Tasks and routines that were once simple for the grandparents may become more stressful and complicated as the grandparents may move at a slower pace in movement related activities and are now responsible for an overly active grandchild with autism. Simple tasks such as shopping for groceries can become stressful as the grandchild with autism pulls food items off of the shelves or lines up grocery items across the floor of the store. Routines that were once in place for the grandparents can become out of wack or quickly changing when a grandchild with autism is part of the extended family structure. For example, grandparents may be used to sleeping with a set scheduled time to go to bed, when a grandchild with autism has disrupted sleeping routines with irregular sleep patterns. This disruption of routines and simple household tasks can make a household more stressful to complete daily routines and tasks.

Appreciation of Pets and Animals

Grandparents and grandchildren with autism can also have positive experiences as they may both seek companionship from pets. As the grandparents seek to have pets as a companion they sometimes use the pet as a focal point in the home or to get attention off of all of the medical woes and financial worries. The pet can provide a relaxing comfort to the grandparent to reduce stress and relate better to other household members. Grandparents do have to supervise young children with autism as they may not understand if they are hurting the pet or reacting in a way that irritates or agitates the pet.

Grandchildren with autism can also find comfort from pets. There have been hints that grandchildren with autism can increase their awareness of the environment around them by having a pet. Perhaps it is because the grandchild bonds in a special way with the pet and this may increase social interaction with others through the special pet relationship.

Communication Struggles

A big similarity between grandparents and grandchildren with autism is that both may be struggling to communicate with others in some way. The grandparents may not hear as well today as when they were younger. Their words can be mumbled from false teeth or slurred from taking various medications. The grandparent's train of thought may impact communication as their ability to hold a conversation may be difficult to follow as topics go in many directions.

The grandchild with autism may also struggle to communicate in a way that grandparents understand. A grandparent may want the grandchild with autism to 'look them in the eye' and may not understand a grandchild's fleeting or limited eye contact with others. The grandchildren with autism may not be able to find the words to say or describe their feelings. As a result, the grandchild with autism is seeking to communicate in other nonconventional ways such as various vocalizations or high pitched sounds.

The Autism Journey is Ongoing

Grandparents are facing a new journey in understanding the unique characteristics of the grandchild with autism. Both the grandparents and grandchildren are learning to find comfort in their new environment together. The grandparents are learning to cope with changes related to the stages of aging and growing older, while the grandchild is often responding to early interventions, new behavior approaches and learning to communicate in a functional and practical way. Both the grandparents and the grandchild have needs that can complement each other and that will need to be addressed in understanding autism issues and concerns. One thing for certain is that the journey in understanding autism is ongoing for both the grandchild and the grandparents.

CHAPTER 2

POOR TESTING EXPERIENCE & AUTISM

Grandparents may quickly be put into a position to get some type of services, evaluation or testing for the grandchild to see if he or she qualifies for a special education eligibility in autism.

Whenever young children are put into an unfamiliar testing situation there is always a chance that a grandchild may look autistic even if he or she does not have autism. Traits and characteristics of autism may come out if the grandchild simply lacks the skills to participate. Can you imagine a grandchild approached by a new (strange) person who is asking him or her to do something? Well this happens many times when a grandchild who lacks the skills to do something may easily turn away, withdraw or simply run out of the room. The first response of some professionals would immediately be to think of the possibility of autism, but on a closer thought this could just be a grandchild in an unfamiliar place who does not want to participate socially with people he or she does not know.

Time of Testing

Many grandchildren can have a poor testing experience because of the time of the testing. The grandchild at home may be used to sleeping late and suddenly is disturbed, put into a car and driven across town to some new unfamiliar office to be tested. This particular time of testing may cause the grandchild to not initiate in a way that the grandchild could normally participate with others. This could give a distorted picture of the grandchild's initiation skills because the time of testing was such a distraction from his or her normal routine. The professionals testing the grandchild may need an explanation of this from the grandparents to better understand the grandchild's behavior on the day of the testing.

Behavior during Testing

Behavior concerns can occur in the testing session as it is an unfamiliar environment for the grandchild. The most notable behavior often noted in reports seems to be the refusal behaviors. The grandchild may refuse to do a requested instruction by simply not choosing to follow a simple direction. However, refusal behaviors can escalate to shouting 'no,' crying, hitting, throwing objects and having a full blown tantrum. Some professionals would immediately suggest autism, but other professionals would step back and look if the grandchild's behavior and tantrums were purposeful or directed at others. The grandparents are important reporters of the grandchild's behavior in the home setting.

Out of Routine Testing Experience

The 'out of routine' encounter of testing seems to be a factor in the testing experience. Often grandparents will comment that the grandchild 'never acts this way' and they are really surprised at the grandchild's reaction to the professionals and testing activities. A grandchild who may have fairly good social interaction skills and plays well, suddenly presents as an upset grandchild who is avoiding social contact and refusing to communicate with professionals after numerous attempts is a big concern for grandparents. This 'out of routine' testing experience can be an important consideration for some grandparents.

Grandparents Expressing Testing Concerns

Grandparents may even need to express their concerns to possibly stop the testing, reschedule another assessment or ask for additional observations at preschool or in the home. The goal for many grandparents is to make sure the professionals have a realistic picture of the grandchild. The testing experience in a new place with a new routine may not fully show the grandchild's full abilities to communicate and socially interact with others. Again, caution would be noted if autism concerns as well as testing observations were not fully documented by the professionals.

CHAPTER 3

SICKNESS & AUTISM

Grandparents may sometimes become confused about autism when the grandchild is sick. This is not that uncommon as sometimes professionals get confused in the same way. Years ago I once heard some professionals talking who thought a child looked autistic when he was actually sick. As I considered this, I realized that a sick or ill child could easily exhibit some characteristics of autism.

Look at the following examples:

Turning Away from Activities

A sick grandchild may turn away or avoid a direct request or task when not feeling well. A grandchild with autism may turn away from a direct request to avoid social interaction.

Avoiding Eye Contact

If a grandchild is sick he or she may avoid eye contact. As a grandchild feels better, he or she may exhibit more eye contact. A grandchild with autism characteristics may avoid eye contact, have minimal eye contact or have fleeting eye contact with others across settings.

Tantrums

A tantrum can be a characteristic of autism as a grandchild resists a change of routine, but it can also be seen in a sick child. A grandchild who wants to go home may tantrum because he or she wants to rest or go to bed.

Social Cues

A grandchild who is well may notice social cues, where a sick grandchild may not respond to social requests or pick up on a social cue or gesture. Although a grandchild with autism may not respond to his or her mother's facial expression, a sick grandchild may not smile or respond to a person's smile since he or she is not feeling well. A sick grandchild may only respond to a few people if his or her needs are not being met, particularly if the grandchild needs something, but doesn't have the language or communication skills to ask for it. A grandchild with autism may only go to one familiar person and not gesture or communicate with others in a room or around a table.

Motion Activities

A sick grandchild may engage in motion activities to distract from not feeling well. For instance, a grandchild may rock back and forth or whirl around to stop thinking about being sick. A grandchild with autism may engage in a motion activity for a longer period of time, where a sick grandchild may cease the activity as he or she starts to feel better.

Withdrawal

A grandchild may withdraw from activities, resist being touched and not participate with others when he or she is feeling sick and wants to be alone. A sick grandchild may not want to play with a group or children and he or she may retreat to a quiet place to avoid active activities. A grandchild with autism may withdraw or crawl under a table as a way to comfort him or herself.

An ill grandchild may stare or seem distance from others as he or she meditates and rests quietly to recover from an illness. The sick grandchild may want to meditate or watch a movie alone in the bed room to recuperate from sickness. A grandchild with autism may stare at particular objects for longer periods to watch a toy movement or spinning motion of an object. At other times a grandchild with autism may withdraw into a corner to avoid social contact with family members or friends.

Final Note

It is easy to see where a grandparent could confuse the behaviors and actions of sick grandchild with a grandchild who actually has autism.

CHAPTER 4

COVERING EARS & AUTISM

Many grandparents are quick to determine that a grandchild has autism if the grandchild covers his or her ears. However, grandparents, parents, guardians and professionals must use caution before they make a quick judgment about a child's action of covering ears.

Let's look at a few examples of young grandchildren's behavior related covering ears:

Defiant Behavior-Some grandchildren with emotional and behavioral issues may cover their ears as a way of saying "I don't want to hear you anymore" or simply "I'm not listening to you."

Sound Sensitivity-There are grandchildren with sensitivity to loud sounds or noisy environments. Some grandchildren (and even adults) cover ears to large amounts of auditory stimulation.

Anxiety-There are some grandchildren who appear as anxious or nervous so they put their hands over the ears to block out the loud noise or sounds in the area. A scary moment at a theme park may cause anxiety and a grandchild may calm down if he or she covers his or her ears for a brief moment.

Illness-A grandchild may cover his or her ears in order to indicate to the grandparent that the grandchild is experiencing an ear ache or pain in the ear or on one side of the face or head. Therefore, the grandchild is covering the ears to indicate to another person or communicate about the pain.

Coping Mechanism-Ear covering can be as simple as having a coping mechanism to deal with the surroundings. The grandchild may cover ears to indicate that he or she is overwhelmed by a situation or event. The grandchild may want to cover his or her ears as a reaction for getting into trouble or being corrected by the grandparent or an adult. Sometimes a grandchild may cover ears to show an uncomfortable feeling related to being embarrassed or not wanting to be approached by a teacher, caregiver, staff member or unfamiliar person.

Some questions to consider in relating ear covering to possible autism or developmental delays may include:

Is the ear covering repetitive and intensive or just happening occasionally?

Is the ear covering related to typical loud sounds (like thunderstorms or a loud siren) or is the ear covering more frequent to even noises that aren't particularly loud or that other people would not consider loud noises?

Is the ear covering an attempt to play with noise sounds noticing that covering ears changes the sounds of the noises in an experimental or curious way?

Is the ear covering a frequent occurrence with intensity or simply a reaction at times to a particular noise or event?

The topic or ear covering is brought up frequently during early childhood assessments and immediately the eligibility of autism is brought to the forefront as the assessment considerations. Professionals and grandparents must be cautious on the topic of ear covering and really look at how the grandchild is responding to the environment and surroundings. Is the grandchild communicating a need, a want or just frustration by covering the ears? Should the assessment team notice this as part of a grandchild's developmental delays or is there a more serious communication and socialization related disorder such as autism? The covering of ears is not always an easy question to answer.

CHAPTER 5

IS MY GRANDCHILD AUTISTIC?

As a school psychologist evaluating young children for developmental delays and autism concerns I have seen a change in who is bringing the children into the testing office. In the past, it was the young parents, but gradually a change has occurred and now an older population is bringing in the young children for assessments. This older population comes in many forms. I have seen fathers as old as seventy who had remarried and started a second family with a younger wife. I have seen grandparents who are the primary caregivers in situations where they totally take on the 'parent or guardian role.' There are also situations where the grandparents are giving 'partial care' of the grandchildren by providing childcare support for their working adult children.

A grandparent shows up at an early childhood diagnostic center full of crying, screaming and overly active children and immediately thinks **'*what am I doing here*?'** The grandparent statements start coming out with a little phrase like **'I'm too old for this.'** The grandparent may vent some frustration as he or she says **'I don't know why my grown children can't take care of their own kids.'** It is not uncommon for there to be some emotional reactions by grandparents and seniors raising grandchildren with autism concerns.

Grandparents and Grandchildren with Similar & Different Issues

Lots of Appointments

The issues are obvious as grandparents and older adults are dealing with some of the same issues of the special needs grandchildren at the same time. Of course, the grandparents may have a need for more doctor appointments as health issues are impacted by the aging process. The grandchild with autism may also need to go to physicians and specialists related to autism, but also the grandchild may have other health needs, therapy appointments, early intervention appointments and other appointments to develop educational programs.

Impact on Budget and Plans

There are also differences in how grandparents and young grandchildren view the recreational aspects of life. Recreational activities are impacted for the senior as well as the special needs child. The retired grandparent may have some resentment for not getting to take that long planned cruise or exotic retirement vacation. Financial burdens of the extra cost of food and clothing may also be a burden on a much more limited retirement income. A grandchild who needs any specialized autism therapy that may also be a burden on the senior's budget. At the same time, the grandchildren start wanting their own recreational activities of movies, fast food, water parks and general somewhat expensive amusement parks. As the numbers of children diagnosed with autism is growing the grandparents must deal with some new issues they may not have had to address in their lives.

Behavior Problems

The senior population often at times has the advantage of experience of having their own children or working with children in some way. Many times grandparents will comment that they have raised many children, but this grandchild with autism is different. Techniques and strategies that worked with the other children and grandchildren do not always work with the grandchild who has autism.

Lack of Communication Skills

Grandparents may wonder how their grandchildren can lack communication skills when the child is raised in a verbal environment filled with talking and language. If the grandchild would just answer the question or respond it would give the grandparents a glimpse of hope. The grandparents are not always equipped or have the strategies to help the grandchild develop practical communication skills.

Socialization Issues

The grandparent may also notice the young child with autism lacks social interaction skills with others. Grandparents may have had a hard time understanding why a young grandchild withdraws from a group of children or is fearful of other people. Grandparents may have observed their grandchildren and noticed the grandchild is totally unaware of others in the room or refuses to join a group of children playing on a playground. Grandparents are often clearly frustrated by the grandchild's lack of play skills. The grandparents who love to express affection with hugs and kisses may not understand a grandchild with autism who resists any type of affection or physical contact.

Sensory Concerns

The grandparents who were raised to 'eat everything on their plates' may get upset when a grandchild with autism is very picky about foods. Some young grandchildren with autism are very picky or selective about the texture of foods or only eating very specific things. There are also other sensory issues where the grandchild may lick or mouth objects or smell many objects before playing with a toy or using the object. The grandparents may have not been exposed to grandchildren with unique sensory issues.

Unusual Behaviors

There may also be frustration for grandparents as they see a grandchild's unusual behaviors, interests or rituals. Grandparents may not understand why a grandchild is lining up toys or objects across the living room floor. These grandchildren with autism concerns may spin objects over and over until grandparents react with anger or outbursts. The grandparents may also have frustration by a grandchild's restricted interest in one toy or object and may not understand why the grandchild won't play with all of the toys. Grandparents can become quickly frustrated because many of these unusual behaviors seem annoying and cause stress in the senior's household.

Help for Grandparents Raising Grandchildren with Autism!

Grandparents dealing with grandchildren with autism can ease some of the frustration by looking at a few strategies:

Get Autism Information

Autism is a very publicized disorder. There is literally tons of information in many forms on autism. Not only are there hundreds of books on autism, but there are numerous websites and blogs that talk about autism concerns and frustrations. Grandparents of grandchildren with autism often share their personal experiences and what types of things have helped grandchildren with autism.

Become Aware of Local Autism Support

Grandparents may not always be aware that many communities have well organized autism support groups that can provide a listening ear and essential autism information to exchange. Some of these support groups can suggest agencies that provide services for grandparents to learn information on 'parenting' grandchildren with autism. The autism support group can make suggestions if the grandparent needs help to advocate for the best interest of the grandchild with autism concerns.

Check Out Early Intervention

When grandparents spot that a grandchild is struggling with communication and social interaction they may want to check with early intervention services in the local community. Many early intervention service agencies provide developmental specialists and speech therapists who can work with the grandchild at a young age. These specialists can pinpoint the grandchild's strengths and weaknesses and often will make comments and suggestions on how the grandchild is progressing in his or her development. Theses specialists may notice red flags or signs of possible autism or developmental delays as well as make referrals for further testing and evaluation.

Respite Care

Many grandparents are unaware of respite care services in the local communities to help relieve the grandparents for a few hours of time. In cultures where you always watch your own kids this might be a new idea. This respite type of care for the grandchild with autism can let grandparents breath a little and have extra time for doctor's appointments, going to the bank or just having some quiet time for reflect on life. This is important because grandchildren with autism can not always be left with anyone. As a result, grandparents may keep the grandchild with autism with them all of the time and may not understand the grandparents need 'alone time' away from the grandchild to take a brief break.

Get a Multi-Team Autism Assessment

A grandparent who has questions or concerns about a grandchild's behavior or communication should definitely seek a multi-team assessment and evaluation for possible autism, developmental delays and other concerns. Sometimes grandparents sense the grandchild may have autism and at other times they notice the grandchild just does not seem to be responding to social and communication cues. The grandparent should start expressing these concerns to professionals in the community. Some grandparents are financially able to get help from medical professionals, but other grandparents usually find help through early childhood agencies or the local school district where there may be an early childhood clinic that provides an educational eligibility for autism or developmental delays.

Get A Referral for a Multi-Team Assessment

The referral process for a multi-team evaluation occurs in several different ways. There are times the grandparents simply call the early childhood clinic and do a referral for the grandchild by expressing concerns. Sometimes the physician makes the referral to the school district to get the grandchild assessed or at other times the early intervention specialists may refer the grandchild to the school district for additional testing and evaluation.

Fill Out Paperwork

Filling out forms for the grandchild's multi-team assessment can be a burden for some grandparents as they struggle personally with vision, hearing or motor issues in holding a pencil. There are times when the grandparents may need to request assistance with this paperwork from a social worker, an office assistance or some type of support staff. Grandparents may be asked to fill out some paperwork and are usually asked to bring in any medical reports with a diagnosis from medical or other professionals who have worked with the child. Once this initial paperwork is completed, the grandparent will give consent for the testing to be completed for the grandchild.

Testing Process

Following the consent for testing, the grandparent will work with a variety of professionals answering interview questions, completing questionnaires, checklists and letting professionals observe and work with the grandchild. As part of this testing process, the grandchild and the grandparent will usually talk to a special education teacher (often for intake) and then see a school psychologist, school nurse and a speech and language therapist. If needed, the grandchild may also see a vision and hearing specialist, an occupational therapist (especially if there are feeding or sensory issues) and possibly a physical therapist. Following the assessment, an eligibility meeting will be scheduled to discuss the results, see if the grandchild is eligible (or not) for the special education school programs and then design a program to help the young grandchild transition into the preschool and school setting.

The grandparents will be provided with lots of information related to autism, developmental delays or other conditions or impairments where the grandchild may need educational support.

If the grandchild is eligible for services, the program will be designed and placement will be discussed with the grandparents as to whether the grandchild needs a specialized autism program, a community based type of class or other community and educational resources that will support the grandchild's educational needs. There are professionals who can support the grandparents through this process as an advocate, social worker, developmental specialist or other agency support to make this process as smooth as possible for the grandparent and grandchild.

Seek to Understand Your Grandchild with Autism

Sometimes grandparents think a grandchild doing repetitive or unusual things is just being annoying to family members. However, if grandparents can change their way of thinking about the grandchild with autism it could shine a new light on the situation. For example, a grandchild with autism may do something over and over because it is a calming or relaxing thing that actually comforts the grandchild. If grandparents can understand why the child does this unusual behavior it can help them realize the grandchild's needs and how the grandchild regulates and processes various types of information and experiences. Grandparents need to continue to love their grandchildren and know there is support and programs to assist them in this journey to understand grandchildren with autism.

RECOMMENDED READING FOR AUTISM

Peterson, S. (2014). Questionable Autism

The book ***Questionable Autism*** involves looking at professional, parenting, research and testing issues related to autism. Numerous questions are developed to consider the broad impact of autism topics for both parents and professionals. Author ***Susan Louise Peterson*** weaves her experiences as an educator and school psychologist for young children into a discussion of some of the major issues impacting the field of autism. ***Questionable Autism*** includes many real world examples related to parenting topics, field issues and general practices in the area of autism. ***Questionable Autism*** has opened the door for broader discussions in the field of autism.

Peterson, S. (2013). Is My Child Autistic or Delayed?

Is My Child Autistic or Delayed? is a book written for parents and professionals to explore autism concerns and developmental delays in children. The book is written by ***Susan Louise Peterson***, a school psychologist who has conducted over 1000 assessments on young children with possible developmental delays and autism concerns.

The book is parent friendly written in easy to understand language. Parent concerns in the areas of communication, stereotyped behaviors, social interaction, unusual behaviors and daily living are presented with a school psychologist's perspective of the concern. The book is also geared to help professionals as it gives an overview of autism characteristics. ***Is My Child Autistic or Delayed?*** even discusses the 'wrong reasons' a parent may want a diagnosis of autism for a child. The multidisciplinary team approach is discussed in the decision making process of whether a child is delayed or has autism characteristics. ***Is My Child Autistic or Delayed?*** gives a nice overview of both parent and professional concerns. Parent concerns in the book include topics such as the type and timing of a referral, cultural issues related to autism, inconsistent living patterns and medical concerns of the child. There is a look at the child's 'purposeful behaviors' to understand delays or autism characteristics. Professional concerns examined in the book include the type of training of the professional, the type of autism assessments and the types of information and behaviors reported that may influence the decision making process of whether a child is autistic or delayed. ***Is My Child Autistic or Delayed?*** is a wonderful resource for parents (and professionals) beginning the process of an educational assessment for possible autism concerns and developmental delays.

INDEX

H

I

M

O

P

R

AFTERWORD

Having had the wonderful experience of working with thousands of parents and grandparents going through the educational eligibility process I have seen both frustration and acceptance of having or raising a child or grandchild with autism. Part of the process is in understanding why the child or grandchild behaves or communicates in a certain way. The other part of the process comes in understanding ways to help the young child or grandchild in the home and then supporting the child or grandchild in the educational setting. The help usually doesn't come from one person, but from a variety of supportive people such as other parents and grandparents that are going through the same autism challenges, from caring professionals that want to help the child or grandchild, from a teacher who says a kind word or notices a strength or major accomplishment the child or grandchild has made and sometimes from a stranger or unfamiliar person who gives a comforting word or understanding comment to help parents and grandparents through the challenging time of raising a child or grandchild with autism.

CPSIA information can be obtained
at www.ICGtesting.com
Printed in the USA
BVHW031356230519
549124BV00001B/176/P